Bless That Wonderful Name

TIMELESS HYMNS, PRAISE SONGS, AND GOSPEL FAVORITES FOR SENIOR CHOIR

Arranged by Marty Parks

with Optional Script

 Lillenas PUBLISHING COMPANY

KANSAS CITY, MO 64141

CONTENTS

I Will Sing Of the Mercies

Psalm 89:1

JAMES H. FILLMORE
Arranged by Marty Parks

7

O Lord, How Wonderful

MOSIE LISTER
and KEN BIBLE

MOSIE LISTER
Arranged by Marty Parks

Bless The Lord, O My Soul

Based on Psalm 103

MARTY PARKS
Arranged by Marty Parks

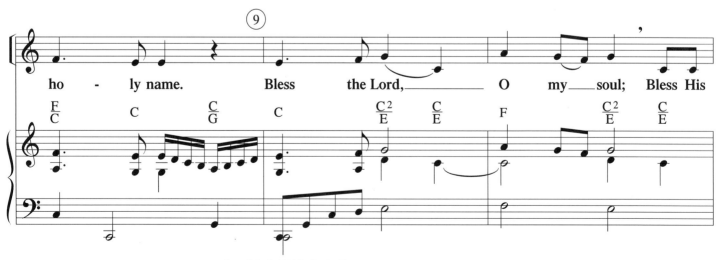

CD: 14

CD: 15

Come, Thou Fount of Every Blessing

ROBERT ROBINSON

Traditional American Melody
Arranged by Marty Parks

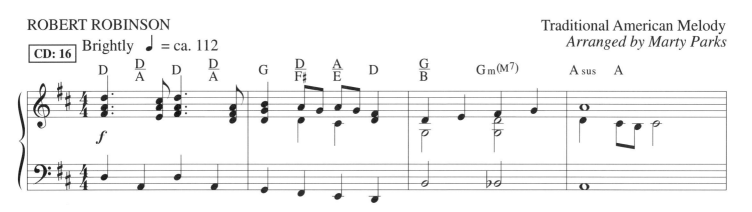

Cleanse Me

J. EDWIN ORR

Maori Melody
Arranged by Marty Parks

30

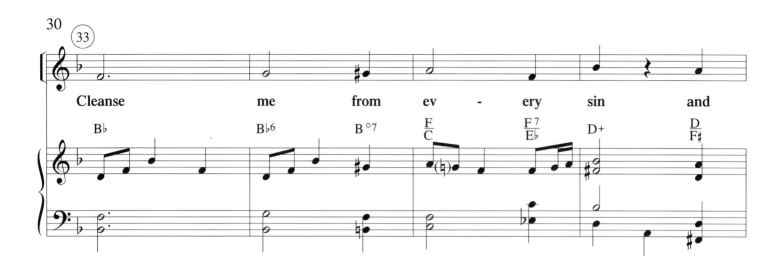

Cleanse me from ev - ery sin and

B♭   B♭6   B°7   F/C   F7/E♭   D+   D/F♯

set me free.

G   G7   C7   F2

CD: 23

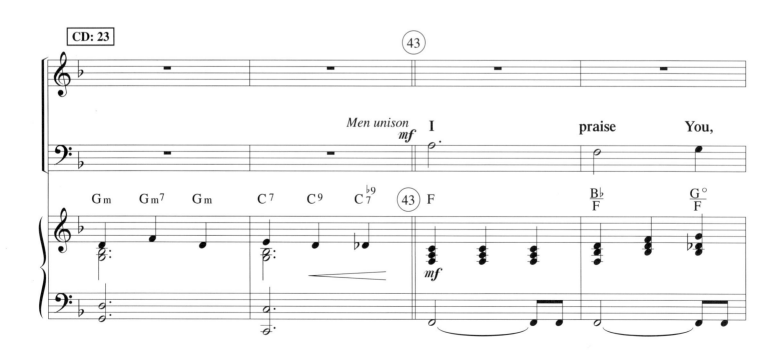

Men unison
mf I   praise   You,

Gm   Gm7   Gm   C7   C9   C7♭9   F   B♭/F   G°/F

mf

Bless That Wonderful Name

Traditional
Arranged by Marty Parks

42

CD: 31

The Longer I Serve Him

with
I Will Serve Thee

Words and Music by
WILLIAM J. GAITHER
Arranged by Marty Parks

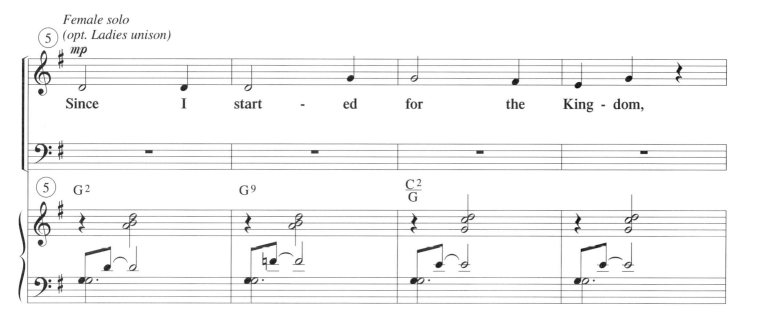

Since I start - ed for the King - dom,

since my life He con - trols;

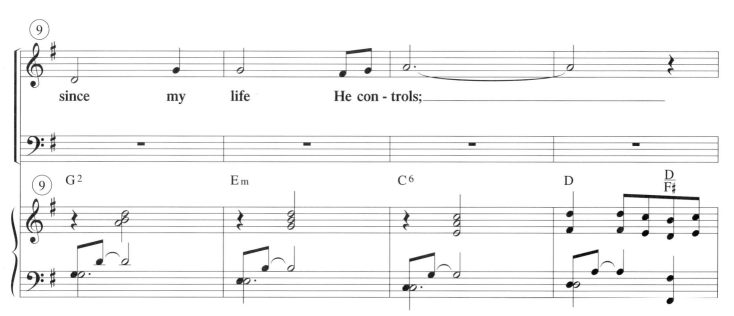

46

Male solo (opt. men unison)

Since I gave my heart to Je - sus, The

long - er I serve Him, the sweet - er He grows.

CD: 34

Duet
(Opt. 2 part choir)

The long - er I serve Him the sweet - er He

48

Peace in the Midst of the Storm

Words and Music by
STEPHEN R. ADAMS
Arranged by Marty Parks

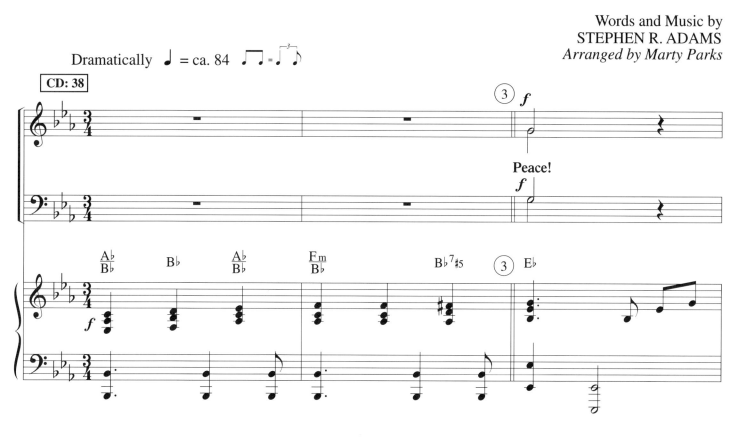

54

56

CD: 40

CD: 41

storm.

E♭   A♭/E♭   E♭
decresc.

Choir unison (opt. solo)
mf   (47)

When my bod - y   has been bro - ken,   'til it's
mf

A♭/E♭   (47) E♭   A♭/E♭
mf

(51)

wracked   in mis - er - y,   When all the doc - tors   shake their

B♭/E♭   E♭   B♭/D (51) Cm²   Cm

Je - sus rides in my ves - sel, so I'll fear no a - larm; He gives me peace in the midst of the storm.

62

Be Still And Know

Psalm 46

Anonymous
Arranged by Marty Parks

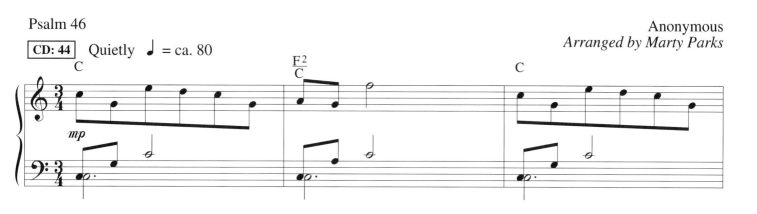

Be still____ and know that I____ am

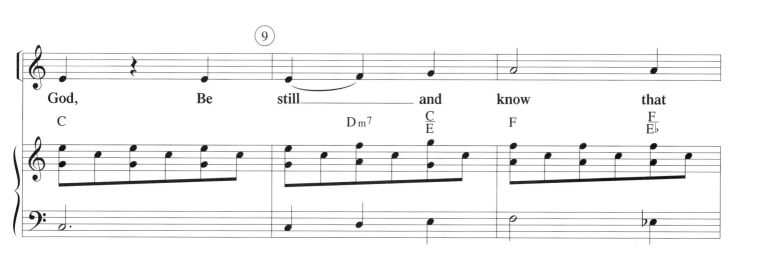

God, Be still_____ and know that

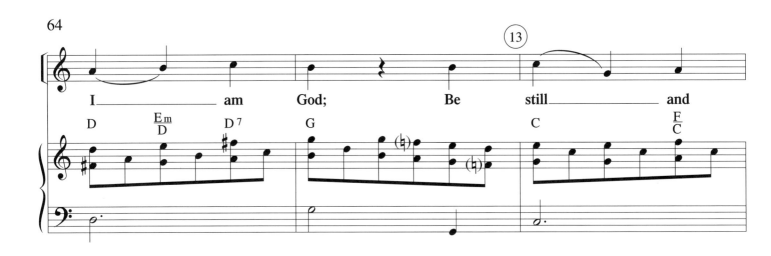

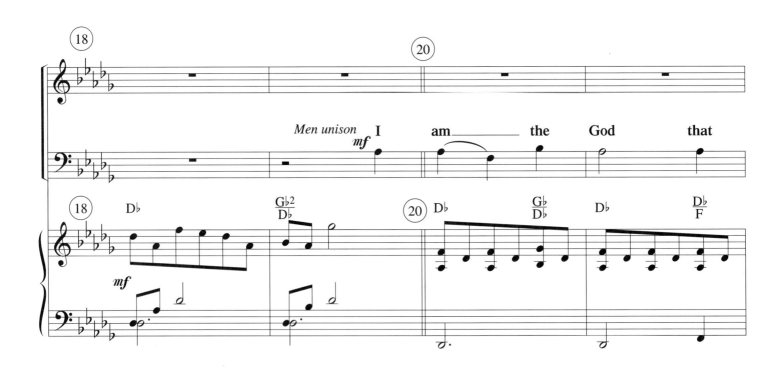

*or "healeth"

Just Over in the Gloryland

JAMES W. ACUFF

EMMET S. DEAN
Arranged by Marty Parks

70

Script

The following are optional narrative scripts that my be included as introductions to individual songs, or combined to create a musical based on God's unfailing love.

NARRATOR: The book of Psalms, the "hymnal" of ancient Israel, speaks as clearly today as it did when it was first written. In it we find outbursts of joy, sorrowful laments and grand expressions of praise. Woven throughout these 150 psalms is the unifying theme of God's unfailing love.

I WILL SING OF THE MERCIES OF THE LORD

NARRATOR: In our day and time, the word "wonderful" is used to such an extent that it's lost some of its original intent. Something described as wonderful should be viewed as inspiring us so that we are filled with awe, amazement and a certain joy in the discovery. In other words, filled with wonder.

Scripture uses the word in a variety of ways. God's deeds are described as wonderful, as are His love and His statutes or laws. Of course, Jesus was named the Wonderful Counselor in anticipation of His earthly ministry.

Perhaps it's time to rediscover the "wonderfulness" of God.

O LORD, HOW WONDERFUL

NARRATOR: When we "bless" God, we are recognizing His worthiness to receive the honor, adoration and praise that's due Him. That's why the Psalmist declared, "Bless the Lord, O my soul; and all that is within me bless His holy name." *(Psalm 103:1)*

Will we ever tire of singing about the Lord's great compassion and His endless mercies?

BLESS THE LORD, O MY SOUL

NARRATOR: As we bless God with our worship and praise, He in turn blesses us with loving-kindness and tender mercy. None of this is because of our own righteousness, but because of His great love. The "Fount of Every Blessing" is truly deserving of our heartfelt gratitude and our endless devotion.

COME, THOU FOUNT OF EVERY BLESSING

NARRATOR: King David, fully aware of his sinful condition, wrote, "Have mercy on me, O God, according to your unfailing love; according to your great compassion blot out my transgressions. Wash away all my iniquity and cleanse me from my sin." *(Psalms 51:1-2)* He also offered this prayer, "Search me, O God, and know my heart; test me and know my anxious thoughts. See if there is any offensive way in me, and lead me in the way everlasting." *(Psalms 139:23-24)*

May we, even today, echo the Psalmist's words.

CLEANSE ME

NARRATOR: Names mean something. In scripture, when God changed someone's name, it was because of some event He'd led them through or some purpose He had in store for them. And when God chooses to reveal His names to us, He is telling us something of His character. This is never so evident as in the names He gave us for His Son– Wonderful Counselor, Mighty God, Everlasting Father and Prince of Peace. *(Isaiah 9:6)*

BLESS THAT WONDERFUL NAME

NARRATOR: Joshua's famous declaration is well-known to most of us– "Choose for yourselves this day whom you will serve...as for me and my household, we will serve the Lord." *(Joshua 24:15)* Years and years of walking with God can be a challenge in this fallen world. We would do well to remember His promises– "I will never leave you or forsake you" and "Lo, I am with you always."

David, the sweet Psalmist of Israel, said it best: "I was young and now I am old, yet I have never seen the righteous forsaken." *(Psalm 37:25)*

THE LONGER I SERVE HIM

NARRATOR: One of Christ's most frequent statements to His followers was this– "Peace be with you." Does that seem like a far-fetched idea to you? Are you facing storms and battles that bring you anything but peace? Are you willing and prepared to go up against these turmoils in your own strength?

Or are you able to turn it all over to the One who brings peace...in the midst of life's storms?

PEACE IN THE MIDST OF THE STORM

NARRATOR: It wasn't in the whirlwind. It wasn't in the fire. It wasn't in the earthquake. It came as a gentle whisper– a still, small voice. That's how the word of God came to Elijah.

How easy it is to forget that amid the frantic pace of today's society God often calls us to cease our striving; to listen quietly; to "be still."

BE STILL AND KNOW

NARRATOR: "No eye has seen, no ear has heard, no mind conceived what God has prepared for those who love him." *(I Corinthians 2:9)* Jesus said, "Do not let your hearts be troubled. Trust in God; trust also in me. In my Father's house are many rooms; if it were not so, I would have told you. I am going there to prepare a place for you. And if I go and prepare a place for you, I will come back and take you to be with me." *(John 14:1-3a)*

We've celebrated and sung about God's unfailing love. This unending faithfulness and blessing of our heavenly Father is not just for the "here and now," but also for the "then and there." There's a bright, bright future for the believer...in Glory!

JUST OVER IN THE GLORYLAND

Bless That Wonderful Name

Timeless Hymns, Praise Songs,
and Gospel Favorites for Senior Choir

TIMELESS HYMNS,
PRAISE SONGS,
AND GOSPEL FAVORITES
FOR SENIOR CHOIR

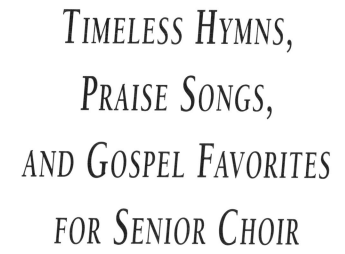
TIMELESS HYMNS,
PRAISE SONGS,
AND GOSPEL FAVORITES
FOR SENIOR CHOIR

Bless That Wonderful Name

Bless That Wonderful Name

TIMELESS HYMNS, PRAISE SONGS, AND GOSPEL FAVORITES FOR SENIOR CHOIR

Bless That Wonderful Name